T0398155

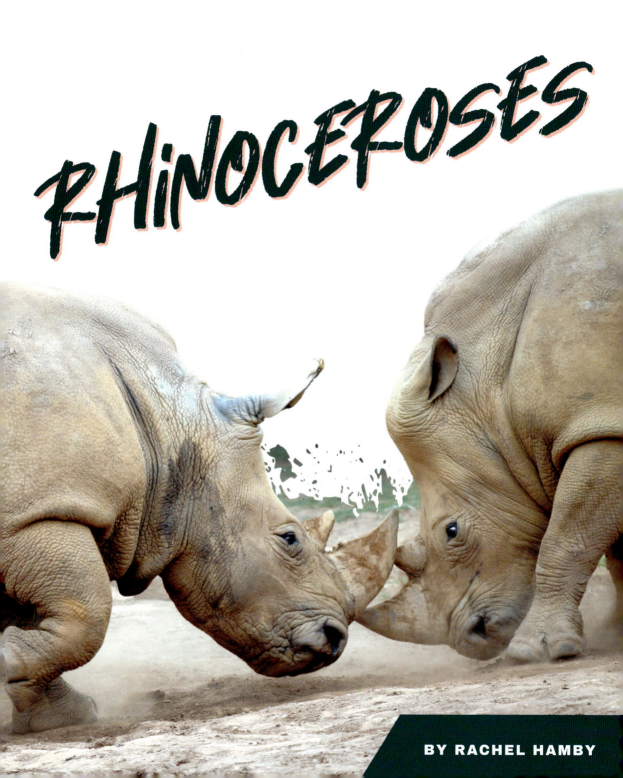

RHINOCEROSES

BY RACHEL HAMBY

Apex is distributed by North Star Editions:
sales@northstareditions.com | 888-417-0195

Produced for Apex by Red Line Editorial.

Photographs ©: Shutterstock Images, cover, 1, 4–5, 8–9, 12, 15, 22–23, 24, 25, 26, 27, 29; iStockphoto, 6, 10–11, 13, 14, 16–17, 18, 19, 20, 21

Library of Congress Control Number: 2022910613

ISBN
978-1-63738-444-2 (hardcover)
978-1-63738-471-8 (paperback)
978-1-63738-522-7 (ebook pdf)
978-1-63738-498-5 (hosted ebook)

Printed in the United States of America
Mankato, MN
012023

NOTE TO PARENTS AND EDUCATORS

Apex books are designed to build literacy skills in striving readers. Exciting, high-interest content attracts and holds readers' attention. The text is carefully leveled to allow students to achieve success quickly. Additional features, such as bolded glossary words for difficult terms, help build comprehension.

TABLE OF CONTENTS

CHAPTER 1

CHARGE!

A rhinoceros is munching on plants. His ears twitch. He hears something. So, he sniffs the air.

Rhinos don't see well. Instead, they use their ears and noses to sense trouble.

He smells another male rhino. The visitor is not welcome. The first rhino wants to defend his **territory**. He snorts and charges.

FAST FACT

Some rhinoceroses can run up to 34 miles per hour (55 km/h).

Rhinos often chase other animals out of their territories.

The two rhinos bump heads. They knock their horns together. The bigger rhino wins the battle. The other rhino runs away.

HUGE HORNS

Rhino horns can grow more than 4 feet (1.2 m) long. Rhinos use their horns to dig for food. They also fight enemies. If a horn breaks off, a rhino can grow it back.

Rhinos can hurt or even kill one another in some fights.

CHAPTER 2

FIVE RHINOS

There are five **species** of rhinoceros. Two species live in Africa. The others live in India, Nepal, and Indonesia.

Javan rhinos live in Indonesia.

White rhinos can weigh up to 6,000 pounds (2,722 kg).

All rhinos have large bodies.

Their legs are short and strong.

Their skin is usually brown or gray.

Large horns grow on their heads.

ONE OR TWO

Different species of rhinos have different kinds of horns. Javan and Indian rhinos have just one horn. White, black, and Sumatran rhinos have two horns. The front horn is usually bigger.

The Sumatran rhino is the smallest. It weighs up to 2,000 pounds (907 kg).

Indian rhinos live in grassy areas that flood.

FAST FACT

Rhinos have lived on Earth for 30 million years.

Rhinos live in many **habitats**.
Asian rhinos live in warm places.
They roam wooded areas near
rivers. African rhinos live on
grassy **savannas**.

Black rhino habitats often have grass and small plants.

CHAPTER 3

RHiNO DiET

Rhinos are **herbivores**. They eat grass, leaves, and fruit. Each species eats different plants. So, rhino mouth shapes vary.

Rhinos can spend several hours each day eating.

A black rhino's pointed lip helps the animal grab plants.

Black rhinos have pointed upper lips. They pull leaves and fruits off trees and bushes. White rhinos have square lips. They grab grass from the ground.

White rhinos can eat 120 pounds (54 kg) of grass a day.

White rhinos eat plants that are low to the ground.

19

Rhinos often rest in the shade of trees.

Rhinos eat in the morning.
They rest in the hot afternoon.
Then they eat again when the
sun goes down.

MUD ALL OVER

Rhinos have thick skin. But they can still get sunburns. So, rhinos take mud baths. The mud coats the rhinos' skin. It keeps them cool. It also protects them from bugbites.

Rhinos roll in mud to stay cool.

CHAPTER 4

LIFE IN THE WILD

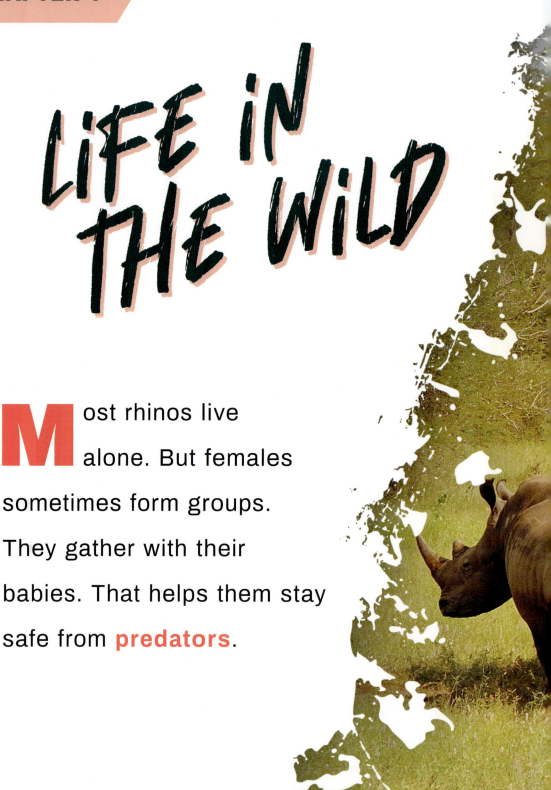

Most rhinos live alone. But females sometimes form groups. They gather with their babies. That helps them stay safe from **predators**.

White rhinos are more likely to live in groups than other rhino species.

Female rhinos have one baby every two to five years. At first, the baby rhino drinks its mother's milk. Later, the mother teaches her baby to eat plants.

FAST FACT

A baby rhino often stays with its mother for two to three years.

Baby rhinos can walk a couple days after they are born.

◀ **Mother rhinos care for and protect their babies.**

Some people use rhino horns for medicine or decorations.

Some rhinos species are **endangered** or almost **extinct**. Humans are their biggest threat. People hunt rhinos for their horns. They also destroy the rhinos' habitats.

PROTECTED PARKS

Today, many rhinos live in parks or preserves. These natural areas are set aside. Rhinos can live there safely. Some parks are even protected by guards.

Kaziranga National Park is home to more than 2,500 rhinos.

COMPREHENSION
QUESTIONS

Write your answers on a separate piece of paper.

1. Write a few sentences explaining what rhinoceroses eat.

2. Which type of rhino would you most like to see in the wild? Why?

3. Which type of rhino has two horns?

   A. Javan

   B. Indian

   C. Sumatran

4. Why would living in groups help rhinos stay safe from predators?

   A. Rhinos could work together to protect one another.

   B. Rhinos could take food from one another.

   C. Rhinos could have more babies each year.

5. What does **threat** mean in this book?

Some rhino species are endangered or almost extinct. Humans are their biggest threat.

    A. something that causes danger
    B. something that is helpful
    C. something that is fun

6. What does **preserves** mean in this book?

Today, many rhinos live in parks or preserves. These natural areas are set aside.

    A. places where people build houses
    B. places where people hunt animals
    C. places where animals can live safely

Answer key on page 32.

GLOSSARY

endangered

In danger of dying out forever.

extinct

No longer living on Earth.

habitats

The places where animals normally live.

herbivores

Animals that eat mostly plants.

predators

Animals that hunt and eat other animals.

savannas

Flat, grassy areas with few or no trees.

species

Groups of animals or plants that are similar and can breed with one another.

territory

An area that an animal or group of animals lives in and defends.

TO LEARN MORE

BOOKS

Adamson, Thomas K. *Rhinoceros vs. African Elephant*.
  Minneapolis: Bellwether Media, 2020.
Duling, Kaitlyn. *Rhinoceroses*. Minneapolis: Bellwether
  Media, 2021.
Murray, Julie. *Rhinoceros*. Minneapolis: Abdo Publishing,
  2022.

ONLINE RESOURCES

Visit **www.apexeditions.com** to find links and resources
related to this title.

ABOUT THE AUTHOR

Rachel Hamby writes poetry, fiction, and nonfiction for kids.
She lives in Washington State with her husband, corgi,
and kids.

INDEX

ANSWER KEY:
1. Answers will vary; 2. Answers will vary; 3. C; 4. A; 5. A; 6. C